Sales Success:
Diagnosing and Prescribing Solutions for Customers

By Kris Patterson

ISBN: 978-0-9881204-4-0
ISBN eBook: 978-0-9881204-9-5

I dedicate this book to the memory of my father Ike Patterson. I constantly use what I learned from him as a salesman and a person. I have also had the privilege of being able to pass on his knowledge to the next generation of salespeople.

I love you Dad.

Kris

TABLE OF CONTENTS

ACHIEVE - Strive to attain your objectives

PERFORM - Meet the challenges

EXPLORE - Broaden your horizons

PURSUE - View every experience as a learning opportunity

REFLECT- Learn from the past to ensure a brighter future

FOREWORD

The remarkable thing about sales is that many people don't even realize that they are in sales. There are the obvious sales persons. Car Salespeople, Advertising Sales Reps, retail sales, and even business to business sales, but there is a larger group of sales people out there that never realize that they directly influence the life of an organization through contact with customers. That is the heart of sales. Customer service people, marketers, even technical service, warranty administration and accounting. Each of these roles in an organization has direct influence over its sales by developing the relationship with the customer.

I used to rail against the idea of "Sales and Marketing" as a single entity or corporate division. Marketing is separate from sales I would say. This came from a desire to edify the important work we were doing and not let the sales department take credit for our successes. Without understanding the place we had in the machine, I tried to take our place out and set it apart, but when you do that, the machine stops turning. Only when all the parts work together in unison can the organization reach its potential.
In that vein, I believe that this book can help many different people in the organization understand the role of sales, and understand the importance that their seemingly unconnected role plays in sales success. A broader view of how all the parts work together helps everyone and that is good for the health of the organization because in our hearts, humans are empathic in nature. We crave understanding of other's experience. In companies where those connections are lacking, we see insular and selfish results, and ultimately failure. In many successful companies, management works hard to give everyone in the organization a broad view of how the company works, and the individual's unique place.

But there is a much more overt purpose to this book. To teach salespeople specific skills and give them the tools to be more successful. Often a sales career begins elsewhere. In a particular individual the innate skills become apparent and management identifies that they would be beneficial in a sales capacity. There are many sales courses out there. There are even Bachelor programs in sales, and there are ways to begin careers in sales, but what if you find yourself in a sales position through a more circuitous route? Through the techniques in this book, you will learn to refine your sales skills and become more successful and a better asset to the organization.

I've come to realize that the learning never stops and one of the keys to continued success is in learning new skills and reinforcing existing ones. There is no neutral gear in business. You are either in drive or in reverse. The direction depends on your commitment to continual improvement. Whether you are a seasoned salesperson, or if you are the accidental salesperson, this book can help you stay in drive.

Christopher Finlayson Marketing and Sales Consultant

INTRODUCTION

Congratulations for getting into a career which I have found to be extremely rewarding. Sales can be one of the highest-paid hardest jobs or the easiest lowest-paying jobs of all time. I've never been more excited to be part of an opportunity career wise where I grow people's businesses and help people succeed. For me there is no bigger satisfaction then the look on a person's face when I've helped them fulfill their dreams of having a successful business which they have worked on for years. There are a tremendous amount of things to be learned in the sales industry which has always been something that appeals to me.

I've been involved in newspaper advertising for many years, selling millions of dollars of ad space. I also gathered a great deal of experience dealing with real estate, car sales and hundreds of other of retail businesses through this occupation. I have also sold millions of dollars of product in the lottery and gaming industry. There was always on the job learning but sometimes that's not enough. I undertook systematic research on how to become in the top 10% of the sales industry and this book represents some of my learning and personal experiences and thousands of hours of research, synthesis and collating. I am very pleased to be able to present this knowledge to you. It is my sincere hope that this book will provide you with the tools to double your sales, increase your happiness and make you feel more successful in life. I hope it will help you on your journey to become part of this exciting career.

You could say I was born into sales. My mother and father were in sales for years. My dad worked at our local radio station for 30 years in the sales, programming and creative departments. My mom also was employed there for years before getting into the publishing arena. I spent many hours in the station as a young person observing the sales process and helping to write and voice radio commercials. I began my actual sales career as a commissioned salesperson for a tourism map company. I then worked in the gaming industry for seven years. This involved a lot of selling as well as exceeding customers expectations. I then moved into newspaper ad sales which afforded me the opportunity to hone my skills even further. I think that everyone is in sales. If you are in business you are in sales. I have had several clients starting out in sales and I have seen their enthusiasm wane after the initial honeymoon period is over. Sales can be tough. I know what it's like to not have the right tools so I thought I would help provide some.

I certainly do not want to pass myself off as an authority however I do feel I have a certain experience which is of value to people in the sales world. I will also mention my crisis line experience only because it helps to explain where some of my skills in dealing with people came from. I believe these experiences are transferable.

I am very pleased to be part of the sales industry. It has allowed me to grow my customer's businesses and to watch them achieve their dreams. I have supported myself and achieved my goals through my assistance in helping my clients achieve their dreams and goals. Sales is a business based on merit, not where you were born or what your previous station in life was. Although sales is considered an entry-level job that in no way implies that it is not a trade. It is a trade that requires constant improvement and work. Sales is about continuous learning, relationship building, listening, and communication and should be worked on daily. I have never worked at a job that offered so much variety and excitement. Sales can be the vehicle to help you achieve all of your goals.

Sales has had a negative stigma attached to it. People think of sales and sometimes they think of a person who would do anything to make a sale. That is not what we wish to become. Integrity and reputation should be of paramount importance to you. Once you have compromised these, it is very difficult, if not impossible to ever regain that level of trust with your client. One of the reasons for me writing this book is that I feel a lot of people discount the sales industry and I find it's gotten a negative reputation which is something I wanted to remedy.

This book is the result of a new awareness of the lack of general sales skills being exhibited in this industry. I first began to notice this lack when I talked to an employee in sales. He came to me expressing his disillusionment with the sales industry. We discussed a lot about the sales field and he was missing some fundamental information on sales basics. He thought that perhaps sales were not for him as he had not had much success. I counseled him to hold on and keep going. He'd only been involved in sales for three months and it is a learning process. This was a moment of revelation for me. I grew up in a household of sales and learned a lot through osmosis. I took this knowledge for granted and perhaps did not put as much of a value on it as I should have. I realize that I had a bit of knowledge that could be used to help people in the sales industry. I also had a huge advantage in that my dad was in the sales industry for more than 40 years. He also constantly studied the sales process. I observed a lot of this information while growing up. I later went into sales myself and I was always asking questions and utilizing his experience and knowledge. I have found myself in the position of mentoring other sales reps and I give them some my dad's wisdom and it becomes a part of their knowledge. Far more important than the sales information I learned from my father was the way to treat people. Relationships are critical in life as well as sales. We spent many hours

2

discussing integrity and safeguarding your reputation. I hope that the readers will use the knowledge and tools here to help their clients.

Working at the newspaper also afforded me the opportunity of working with several junior sales reps. I have found that most sales jobs at best provide mediocre product knowledge and virtually nothing on the process of sales itself. Although product knowledge is important, knowledge of the sales process is equally critical. Through this book I hope to provide some tools and insights into that sales process which will help catapult your career to the next level. I have included examples from my own past through sales in newspaper, online and other forms of advertising.

My goal in this book is twofold. In addition to providing some sales tools, I am also equally concerned with eliminating the negative stigma attached to the sales profession. I feel that the old method of sales has gone away or at least should be hurried on its way. With the improved education of the customer there is no longer a place for manipulative sales. Unfortunately many people have got a negative impression of sales like the slimy salesman or the cutthroat person that would do anything to make a dollar. This is not the form of sales I personally practice nor do I feel it is actually effective in this day and age. I have prided myself on the relationships and rapport I have built with my customers. These relationships have transcended my time at any one place of employment.

My dad, Ike taught me most of what I've learned in the sales industry. But more importantly he taught me how to deal and relate with people. This was a skill I honed through many other jobs especially as a crisis intervention worker, gaming industry worker and several other retail jobs. When writing this book I realized how lucky I was to have a father like Ike. Writing this book led me to reevaluate and revisit some of the sayings that he passed on to me which in turn I have begun to pass on to my colleagues in the sales office. I also took the time to reevaluate my past and found what was useful and what was not useful. Some of the techniques for active listening were derived from my time as a crisis intervention worker. This was a position which gave me an excellent opportunity to hone my communication skills. A lot of what I learned in those classes and on the phone lines directly applies to sales although the stakes are a lot different in this case.

Sales should be the beginning part of any business education. I look upon sales much like the medical profession. Much of what we do as sales people is called needs analysis. This is basically finding out how we can help a customer by figuring out what they need and provide solutions to that problem. Sales is not much more complicated than that. Just as a doctor would never prescribe medication without first doing a diagnosis, a salesperson diagnoses the client's needs before offering a solution. I would also encourage people to realize that everybody in one way or another is involved in sales. Salespeople are the backbone of the economy and drive a lot of change in the world. You should take pride in being a member of this prestigious trade. I think it's an incredible business and I am proud to consider myself a salesperson.

My First Foray into Commission Sales

MODERN SELLING VERSUS OLD SELLING

> "To improve is to change; to be perfect is to change often."
> – *Winston Churchill*

Sales have changed. Sales take longer now and there's more competition for customer dollars. Price comes up earlier in the discussion. If you discuss price out of order in the sales process you will definitely kill the sale. If you are arguing price you have not differentiated yourself properly. Handling the price objection will be a critical skill for sales professionals to master. If you are discussing price you have failed to differentiate yourself and your product. The average is now 4 to 6 calls to make a sale today. There are now many decision-makers instead of a single decision-maker. Customers are more advanced and knowledgeable than ever. There is also more competition than there ever was before.

When I decided to make sales my career I undertook a study of how to systemize sales. This led me to a lot of research and hundreds of books. It took a great deal of time to wade through the nonessentials that were in those books. A lot of what those books were still teaching was the old school sales from the 1950's "Where liars are buyers, close them early, close them often." Very little of the old school sales training focused on rapport building or relationship building. It was always say what it takes to make the sale regardless of if it's true or not. It is my hope that my book will be an antidote to this way of thought.

Sales has changed a lot from the 30s and 40s hard-sell technique, from all the research I've done it looks like relationship selling skills started in the 1970s. By the time the 1980s came we began to include needs analysis.

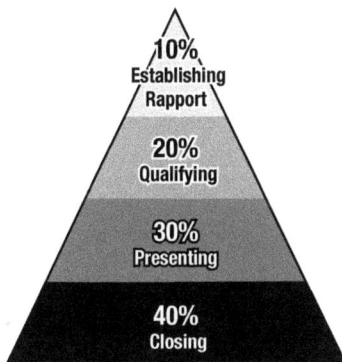

Old method of selling	New method of selling

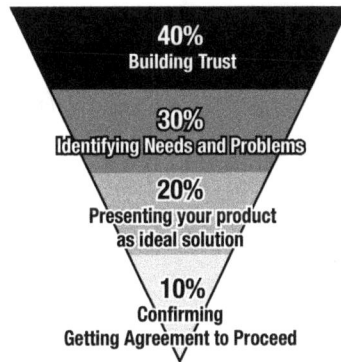

Old method of selling (pyramid, top to bottom): 10% Establishing Rapport; 20% Qualifying; 30% Presenting; 40% Closing.

New method of selling (inverted pyramid, top to bottom): 40% Building Trust; 30% Identifying Needs and Problems; 20% Presenting your product as ideal solution; 10% Confirming Getting Agreement to Proceed.

Customers are much smarter now and better educated every year that goes by. There is no more room for high pressure, manipulative sales. Salespeople today need to be relationship oriented. Customers are smarter than ever which means that salespeople also need to be masters of change, constantly learning. You should be studying sales, relationships, decision-making etc. Remember that the most important ability is responsibility.

Sales is about relationships, take for example the remora fish which has a symbiotic relationship with the shark. It attaches itself to the shark getting a meal by cleaning the shark. Both parties in this relationship benefit, the shark gets clean and the fish gets a meal. This is a great metaphor for the relationship between a sales person and their clients. Customers can increase in value by investing time in building high quality relationships. They can offer referrals and repeat sales. Tell your new customers that you are looking for a long-term relationship.

Credibility is made up of three things:
- trustworthiness,
- competence,
- dynamism and energy.

Technology has not brought the demise of the salesperson. It is actually made every one a salesperson which makes this book that much more important.

CUSTOMER IS KING

> "Always exceed customer's expectations remember there are no roadblocks or traffic jams on the extra mile." ~ *Brian Tracy*

The purpose of business is to create and keep a customer. A profit is the result of running a successful business.

Remember the customer is the boss. This is the one boss you must please. Everything you own they have paid for. He or she buys your car, your home, and your clothes. It is important not to lose sight of this. I have found that no matter how complex things get, when you get away from this core concept, things get out of focus. The good news is that most customers are fair. They can be won back if they are treated well and with the importance that they deserve. They also will bring other customers into your place of business.

I have had some customers who were more difficult than others as I'm sure other salespeople have. I always treat them with the respect and courtesy that they deserve. One of my bosses was famous for saying "Always take the high road" he was very correct and I took this philosophy to heart. When you have a difficult customer don't allow their attitude to affect yours, always conduct yourself professionally and never allow negativity into your attitude.

All customers have bad days like everyone else does. Make sure their time with you is valuable and productive and they will always want to come back.

Negative prejudgment is a big cause of failure in the sales world. Never assume the worth of the customer based on first impressions. I had a client at a jewellery store prejudge a customer at first impression as not worth the time because he was dressed shabbily and was unshaven. A junior sales rep took the time and dealt with him and he was actually a commercial fisherman who immediately upon getting off the boat wanted to buy an engagement ring and other jewellery to propose to his girlfriend. This day turned into a $10,000 sale because a junior rep was willing to take the time with the customer. He also became a regular customer throughout the years.

The future is filled with challenge and excitement and opportunity. There are new horizons in many industries and new sales needs opening up in many industries and specialized fields. Put in the research, always be learning.

The relationships that I have prided myself on building with my customers have led them to describe me in several ways. My clients describe me as feeling like I work for them rather than my company. They view me as an unpaid member of their staff and they know that I care more about their business rather than just making the sale.

Your thought for every moment of work should be what can I do for my customer? Always remember how important the customer is for without them there would be no need for your product or service.

You want to be in business for a long time not just for a few one-shot sales. Develop friendships with customers; they can have a solid foundation especially when based on a salesperson's genuine interest in his customer's welfare.

A company's greatest asset is its reputation. The same applies for sales professionals.

Remember that the customers will decide our success or failure. To satisfy your customer is a central focus which will allow your business to grow.

THE IMPORTANCE OF SERVICE

> "Biggest question: Isn't it really 'customer helping' rather than customer service? And wouldn't you deliver better service if you thought of it that way?" ~ *Jeffrey Gitomer*

Researchers consistently find that it cost five times more to attract a new customer than it does to keep one you already have.

Only four out of every 100 unhappy customers complain to the business, of those that are unhappy 91 % tell their friends and 13 % will tell 20 people or more.

The following list of where customers go will illustrate the importance of service:

Percentage of lost customers:

Died 1 %
Moved 3 %
Buy from or through friends 5 %
Don't like the product service or price 14 %
Poor service or employee behaviour 68 %
Prefer competitor 9 %

Customer service accounts for 68 % of the reasons customers leave. By focusing on good service you set yourself up for a winning experience.

HANDLING IRATE OR ANGRY CUSTOMERS

"Remain calm, serene, always in command of yourself. You will then find out how easy it is to get along." – *Paramahansa Yogananda*

Sometimes it will be necessary to deal with customers who are upset. Give them permission to vent their frustration. It is important to allow the person to vent before trying to solve the problem. The customer needs to be acknowledged before they will listen to your solution. When a person is angry they are not listening rationally because they're hurt or disappointed. It is also important for you to remember that they are not attacking you personally.

CRITICAL SUCCESS FACTORS IN SALES

"The difference between a successful person and others is not a lack of strength, not a lack of knowledge, but rather in a lack of will."
– Vincent T. Lombardi

1) Prospecting
2) Establishing rapport
3) Determining needs
4) Presenting your product as the ideal solution to the customer's need
5) Answering objections or concerns that the customer might have
6) Asking for the order and closing the sale.
7) Follow Through and implementation
8) Getting resale and new sales to referrals to new prospects and customers.

Rank yourself a scale of 1 to 10 in each area. One being very poor and ten being perfect. Your weakest critical success factor determines the limitations with which you can use the others. You should be at least a seven on each area to achieve great success.

PROSPECTING

> "Fish where the fish are" – *Chuck Lamb*

The critical success factors in prospecting are:

1) Identifying prospects
2) Qualifying prospects
3) Telephone skills
4) Getting an appointment
5) Getting past the blockade
6) Getting them to consider changing to your product
7) Getting follow-up meetings

Prospecting is crucial. You should always keep new customers continually coming in. Smaller sales are about quantity seeking as many potential customers as possible, while larger sales are about quality of the prospect.

All prospects are in one of three situations:

1) Has a specific problem and the knowledge of what it is.
2) Has a specific problem but they are unclear about it.
3) They have a problem that doesn't exist at all and they don't need your product or service.

Prospecting is what you use to find out which situation they are in.

a) The goal is to get to the person with a need.
b) Remember to always start with an interview make no attempt to sell.

NEADS Qualification Sequence:

Now find out what they have now
Enjoy what they like about what they have now
Alter: what would you like to see altered
Decision-maker: who in addition to you will be making the decisions?
Solution: if we could find the right solution for your needs would you be in a position to proceed.

Triplicate of choice: don't present them with a choice of fifteen items; pare it down to three choices, the three most likely.

Four questions you need to be able to answer to qualify prospect:

> 1) Does the customer need the product?
> 2) Can the customer use the product?
> 3) Can the customer afford your product?
> 4) Does the customer want your product?

Not everyone is a prospect even if they can buy. Sell strategically. Talk to the right person. Research your customer and their company before you start. Earn the right to meet with the customer. A salesperson is a problem solver. What does your product do for the customer? Look at your product from the customer's point of view and what results will the customers get. Get out of yourself and into the mind of your prospect, what are their difficulties?

Find problems that the customer has and that can be profitable for you and them to solve. This is win-win. The value of the solution presented must be greater than the cost of buying it for the customer. The failure to do this is the reason that most sales fail.

Planning Stage Questions
What exactly is my product or service?
Who exactly is my customer?
Why does my customer buy?
What are my customer concerns?
What is it that makes my product or service appear that of my competitors?
Why is it that my prospect does not buy?
What is my perspective customer buy for my competitors?
What value does he or she perceive from buying from my competitor?
How can I offset that perception and get my competitors customers to buy from me?
What one thing must my customer be convinced of to buy from me rather than someone else?

COMMUNICATION

Emotion comes first backed by logic

Face to face contact with your client is your best sales tool, the second is the phone. One of the biggest mistakes salespeople make is thinking that a telephone can substitute for face-to-face meeting with the prospect.

Our attitude comes across to people through our body language and tone of voice and words. What we say is not as important as how we say it.

In face to face communication the following breakdown with percentages show the importance of non-verbal communication:

> Body language 55%
> Tone of voice 38%
> Words 7%

It's very clear from this breakdown that non-verbal characteristics account for 93% of communication. It does change slightly on the phone because of course they don't have access to non-verbal characteristics. The percentage of what the listener actually receives is 20% words and tone of voice accounts for 80% while on the phone.

Questions can be a powerful tool to encourage dialogue. Remember to ask open ended questions. Open ended questions are questions that cannot be answered with a simple yes or no. Questions are only one half of the communication equation. You must also **LISTEN** to the answer. I have included some sample questions that I have used to encourage discussion.
I would strongly encourage you to come up with a list of about ten questions that you will have prepared and practiced.

To Listen

you
ear
eyes
undivided attention
heart

The Chinese characters which make up the verb "to listen".

Sample Questions:

What motivated you to get started in this business?
When people talk about your business what do they say they like?
Who are you trying to reach?
What's your most profitable product?
Are you bringing in new products?
What is the value of the average customer to you?
Where do you see yourself into the five years?

Another question to ask after you've had your initial meeting with your customer and done a presentation ask them on a scale of 1 to 10 what is your level of interest in doing business with me if they answer 7,8 or 9 you've pretty much made the sale. If they've answered in the low numbers ask them what else you need from me to get to a 7, 8 or 9.

When the last question has been asked say to your prospect say "You know Mr. Customer I've learned a lot today and I want to thank you for taking the opportunity to talk to me, let me tell you what I usually do at this stage. I think we are at the point now where I need to set up another appointment for us, one where I can come back after having sorted through the things I've learned here and show you what we may be able to do for your company is Tuesday at 3 o'clock okay?"

Questions you should ask yourself as a salesperson:

What is the most important psychological benefit your product offers?
How have your customers needs and desires change in the recent past?
What changes have you made to accommodate these changes?
Who is your customer? Who do you have to satisfy to move ahead in your career? Who are your most important customers?
What does your customer consider value?
What specific benefits does your customer get from using your product or service?
Why does your customer buy from you rather than someone else? What do you do especially well for your customer?
What is your area of superiority? What is your area of competitive advantage?
Ask your customers what they perceive to be the special advantage or benefit of dealing with you. You may be surprised

10 questions for establishing rapport:
1) How did you get started in?
2) What do you enjoy most about what you do?
3) What separates your company from your competition?
4) What advice would you give to someone just starting out in your business?
5) What one thing would you do with your business if you knew you could not fail?
6) What significant changes have you seen take place since you started in this industry?
7) What do you see as the coming trends in your business? This question allows the person to speculate.
8) Describe the funniest or strangest experience in your business. This gives them the chance to tell their war stories?
9) What ways have you found the most effective in promoting your business?
10) What one sentence would you like people to use in describing your business?

Paraphrasing:

Paraphrasing is a way of stating what you've heard back to the customer in your own words in order to ensure you've understood what has been said. For example If I have heard you correctly, and then restate what has been said.

Key rule: Listening builds trust and credibility.

PRODUCT KNOWLEDGE

"Knowledge is power and for retailers, product knowledge can mean more sales" – *Shari Waters*

You must know your product inside and out as well as knowing your customers and your territory.

Selling is a key part of a free enterprise system. We help keep the wheels of industry turning and help create income. You should always feel pride in your role. There is a lot of negative connotation to being a salesman. This is ridiculous everyone really is in sales. Everyone is selling something, their talents, their time, themselves, an idea or a way of life.

It helps to sell something you believe in, something that you would personally use and something that provides value to the customer. Being able to sell anything to anyone is more like description of a con man, not the sales professional we aspire to be.

I have worked in the newspaper industry for many years. I am very proud to represent the paper of record in my community. This paper has been part of the community since 1907 and I am pleased to be part of its continuing lineage. I have had the distinct pleasure of being able to help people grow their businesses. I know that my paper is a very effective way of satisfying my customer's needs, so much so that when I launched my first book, I bought an ad personally at full rate to prove that I walk the walk and stand behind my product.

You must possess superior knowledge of your product and service. Know it cold. Gain superior knowledge of the customer's situation. Position your product or service. Show the success of your product or service using testimonial letters from satisfied customers, lists of customers who have used your product or service in the past, photographs of customers using your product or service, which also allows you to discuss the amount of referrals and resales that you get. Don't forget about third-party endorsements. Have people in the community tell stories about the success they've had with your product. Satisfied customers also lower the risk for people to buy from you.

VALLEY SPOTLIGHT

Kris Patterson invites you to celebrate the launch of the new book

"This Was Then with Old Ike"

Thur., Aug. 30 – 7:30 pm
Alberni Valley Museum
Echo Centre

Book Sale
Refreshments

Seating is limited
RSVP 250-723-2181

BEATING THE COMPETITION

> Competition brings out the best in products and the worst in people
> *– David Sarnoff*

Position yourself
Product knowledge
Customer knowledge database
Penetrated to final decision-maker

Positioning yourself is very important. 80% of sales are often based on reputation.
Have you uncovered a problem or need your customer has that your product has solved?
Have you convinced them of their need for your product?
Have you quantified your solution?
Have you demonstrated your professionalism and competence?

Competition appears because of risk. Customers always want to make the best decision. Leave it with me, I need to check with someone else, these phrases mean I want to lower risk, to delay the decision to look for ways to lower the risk. Your goal is to be the preferred option. The best choice overall.

Focus on features and benefits.

1) Determine the decision criteria. On what basis are you going to make this decision?
2) Organize the criteria by importance what is the most important?
3) Compare available options to see which one fits best with the decision criteria?
4) Make a decision which fits best with this process and take action.

Work with the customer and discover which option you provide will best resolve their concerns.

One example you can use is Mr. Customer there is a lot involved here, but your main consideration in this decision is ____ and then state the strengths of your product.

Who is your competition and in this account specifically?

Ask the customer what it is about the competitions offer that appeals to them?

What is your competition it can be other uses for the customer's money and it can also be ignorance in that they don't realize that there's a need that needs to be fixed.

Ask why do your customers buy from your competition? Ask the customers why they buy? What benefit or benefits they perceive that they get from the competition that they don't get from you?

What is it that our company does better than anyone else?

What is it that the competition does better than anyone else?

I have never been a fan of focusing on what my competition is doing. I've always found that it allows the competition to write the rules, it advertises your weakness not your strengths, and it also invites price slashing and deflects customers concerns.

There was a famous basket ball coach named John Wooden he won more NCAA consecutive championships than any other coach. He was interviewed one day and the journalists said how do you do so well especially as he was known as the one coach who never used scouts to see what the opposing team was doing. When he was queried about this he responded by saying when I get my players doing what I know they're capable of doing, it doesn't matter what the other guys are doing. I think this story is a directly applicable lesson that can be used in sales. I do think that you should know and be aware of what the competition is doing but certainly do not allow them to dictate your actions.

Never bash the competition, focus on what you can do.

SELLING AGAINST PRICE

"The bitter taste of poor quality lingers long after the sweet
taste of low price is forgotten" – *Anon*

Seven non-price determinants of each sale:

1) Quality of product which means suitability to what the customer's needs are at that time
2) Delivery: fast dependable predictable
3) Installation: reduces worry if customer has the product installed and it's less work for the customer
4) Terms: What is the down payment how do you do your billing etc.
5) Service you offer after the sale
6) Follow-up support
7) Reputation of company.

Every study shows customers rank price six out of seven in importance. Salespeople are actually often the ones who bring up price. When you are up against price it means you have done a poor job of explaining the value of your products and have not alleviated the customer's perceived risk.

Focus on the customer's needs, keep smiling, work on the relationship, keep asking questions and you will come out ahead.

Risk is the critical factor in sales. Customers fear did they pay too much for the item did you buy the wrong thing, etc. Fear of making a mistake is 80% of why people don't buy.

Price is too high: this should be dealt with asking the customer more about why it is too high. Often the real reason is the prospect has not understood the value of the product or perhaps you have not discovered the prospects true needs.

Price objections these are often knee-jerk reactions to an unexpected expense. Price is seldom the reason to buy anything. Ask people to show you something that they bought solely because it was the cheapest item. Never bring up price until the customer does. Focus the presentation on the value to the customer and what they're getting not on the money you are receiving.

You do not want to be the lowest priced provider. People who buy solely on the basis of price are difficult to deal with, poor sources of referrals and are poor payers who complain a lot and are difficult to deal with. The reasons for price are what is important.

Too many salespeople sell today based on price and not value. Some lower people in a company are only concerned with price because they want to impress their higher-ups by getting a good deal. The top salespeople discuss results to customers and the benefits, you should also.

Position yourself as the best choice rather than the lowest price.

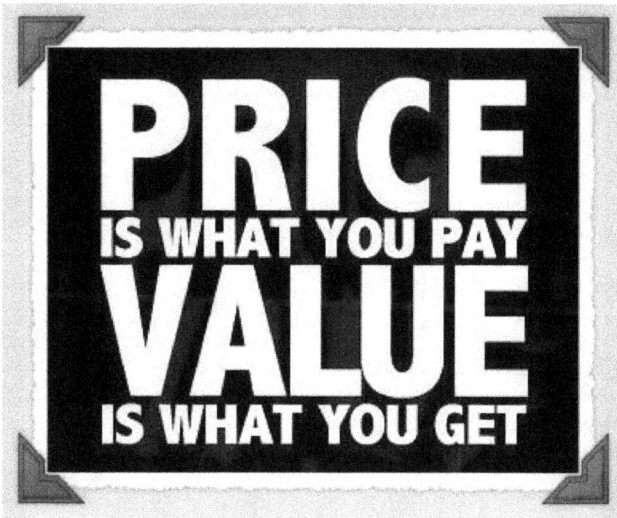

PRICE IS WHAT YOU PAY
VALUE IS WHAT YOU GET

WHY DO CUSTOMERS BUY?

> "Quality in a product or service is not what the supplier puts in. It is what the customer gets out and is willing to pay for. A product is not quality because it is hard to make and costs a lot of money, as manufacturers typically believe. This is incompetence. Customers pay only for what is of use to them and gives them value. Nothing else constitutes quality."
> – Peter Drucker

Many people try to sell products only through logic, but people rarely buy logically. People buy emotionally and then defend their decisions with logic. People love to buy but they hate to be sold. People will pay for want before they pay for need.

Four factors that impact the customer's decision:

1) Size of the sale: Sales today are larger
2) Several people are now involved in the decision process of the sale
3) Products or services have a longer life
4) Whether or not they are a first-time buyer.

Six categories of buying impulses:

1) Security: Monetary gain freedom from financial worry
2) Self preservation: safety and wealth for self and family.
3) Convenience: comfort more desirable use of time.
4) Avoidance of worry: ease of mind, confidence.
5) Recognition from others social status, respectability, the wish to be admired.
6) Self-improvement: spiritual development, hunger for knowledge, intellectual stimulation.

Three greatest motivational factors are:

1) Desire for gain
2) Fear of loss
3) Desire to be loved and to love

There are several types of customers:

Apathetic buyer: they represent 5% of customers and they won't buy no matter what. Extricate yourself as soon as possible.

Self-actualized buyer: they are the 5% of the other side of the spectrum who know exactly what they need and want and if you have that they will buy right away. Sell them exactly what they need and don't try to up sell this type of buyer.

Analytical buyer: they represent 30% of customers. They are the thinkers. They want to know the details accountants and administration people etc. they love the details.

Integrated sales people need to be able to sell to all types of customers. Everybody has their own distinctive style and personality; don't make the mistake of slipping into your style and trying to make the customer conform to you. One of the biggest reasons customers buy is they like their sales rep. Like leads to trust, trust leads to buying, buying leads to relationships.

Negative prejudgment is one of the biggest reasons for losing sales. Deciding in advance if the prospect won't like it and making the decisions for them is a recipe for disaster in the sales world.

The key obstacle to buying is risk. The fear of making a mistake. The fear of poor after sales service. The new method of selling is the antidote to this fear.
Building trust is the most important step in selling.

OVERCOMING OBJECTIONS

> "The number one secret to overcoming price objections is to actively listen to your client and create value that exceeds their expectations" – *John Di Lemme*

There are two types of objections. Minor and major

Minor objections are defence mechanisms used to slow things down. The customer may want or need additional information. Don't argue, don't attack your client when they voice their objections, listen to the objections and discuss the options. I always try to lead clients to answer their own objections. Hear them out, feed the objection back, question the concern, ask for any more objections, and confirm the answers.

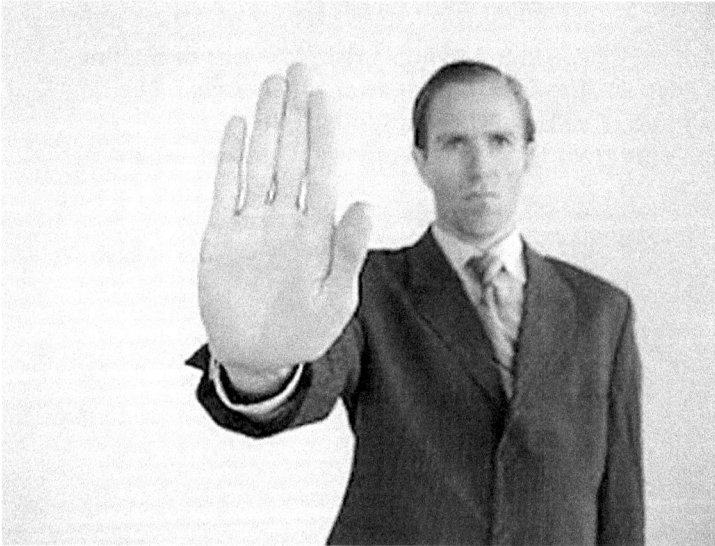

CLOSING

"Every sale has five basic obstacles: no need, no money, no hurry, no desire, no trust." ~ *Zig Ziglar*

Many people are afraid to ask for the sale. I have included several closes in this book not perhaps for you to use, but for you at least to be aware of how other people are selling. I have found if you have done everything right up to this point closing is almost done for you.

Close on the benefits that are most viable to your buyer. Closing is using people's desire to own the benefits of your product, and blending your sincere desire to serve in helping them make decisions that are truly good for them. Many times sales are closed in cars, restaurants, on customers desk, display rooms, and many other places that are actually not designed primarily for closing business, always be ready. Have your closing materials in a permanent spot in your briefcase, car, and office always ready to go. Always use clean new forms and have a calculator with you, do precise figures and never guess.

You must see the benefits, features and limitations of your product or service from your potential buyer's viewpoint.

1) The basic oral close: primarily for industrial, commercial and government sales an example would be what purchase order will be used for this requisition.

2) Basic written close: what address will we be shipping this to? Or you need delivery no later than the 15th let me make a note of that.

3) Pro versus con list this is exactly what it sounds like take a sheet draw a line down the middle with yes on one side and no on the other. Write all the reasons favouring the decision on the yes side with the no side having all the reasons against. After that all you simply do is a tally of the answers. The decision is made for you. This has also been referred to as the Benjamin Franklin close. When I was working in the crisis intervention field we used this tool frequently. We use this tool to allow people to come to a decision themselves rather than being told what to do. I would of course have the customer themselves fill it out rather than you filling it out for them.

4) I want to think it over close: sometimes a customer wants to think it over, to sleep on it. Ask the question just to clarify my thinking what is it that you wanted to think over? Is it the level of service provided? Is it

the product's capabilities? Ask questions that will cause them to tell you how great your product is. Eventually it usually boils down to money problems.

5) Reduction close: when people say something is too much this is where you take the price and you break it down over a year and then break it down by month and week to make the price seem smaller.

6) Puppy dog close: this is where you have the person take the product home to try it out for the weekend. It was originally used to sell puppies in a pet store by allowing the customer to take the dog home for the weekend knowing that people would bond with it and they would not return the dog come Monday.

7) Similar situation close: when you are working with someone who has a concern similar to what you've just overcome you share that story with them.

8) Economic truth close: if you have a superior product you run up against a competitor with a less expensive yet inferior product try this "It's not always wise to make buying decisions by price alone. Investing too little has drawbacks, you risk that the item you've purchased may not give you the satisfaction you are expecting. It's an economic truth that it is seldom possible to get the most by spending the least. It might be wise to add a little to your investment to cover the risk you're taking that the product might not be right for you"

9) I can get it cheaper close: when they say I get it cheaper somewhere else you say that might be true we all want the most for our money. A truth I've learned over the years is that the cheapest price is not always what we want. Most people look for three things when making an investment: quality, service and lowest price. I have never found a company that could provide the finest quality and best service at the lowest price I'm curious for your long-term happiness which of the three would you be most willing to give up?

10) Higher authority close: find someone in the industry that you wish to close on the sale and ask your expert if they are willing to share their knowledge of the product with other noncompeting businesses. Then when talking to your prospect and you have a list of questions, concerns or objections then asked if they know the person you're about to use your authority and make a quick phone call and have your expert go over the questions with your clients.

11) Lost sale close if you've done everything you can possibly do but still think there's a chance on the sale apologize to them and ask what you did wrong and please be candid with me if you ask with sincerity the customer can give you something to work with.

12) The alternate close: would you like this or would you like that give them two options.

13) Authorization sale Close: if you like this I need your authorization take out an order sheet and ask him what the correct spelling of his last name is or confirm his delivery address if they give you the info you have made the decision to buy.

14) Invitational close: If you like this why don't we get started?

A great close to use is: "What would you like me to do now" or "How would you like me to proceed?" I found these to be great ways to get the sale and I've used them many, many times.

Testimonial letters are also great tools because they limit risks with customer.

Most people need help in making decisions because they are afraid of making bad ones. Hesitation leads to indecision.

Ask, the future belongs to the asker.

TIME MANAGEMENT

"Every day man crucifies himself between two thieves – the regret of yesterday and the fear of tomorrow." ~ *Benjamin Disraeli*

Always ask yourself what is the most valuable use of your time right now? Ask yourself is what I'm doing right now leading to a sale.

Always have your day planned the night before, don't leave it to chance. Too many salespeople waste time trying to decide who to call on next. The ability to organize your time is as important as the ability to sell. Keep a daily sales call sheet with what you did and the results. It takes very little time and has personally saved me on more than one occasion. I have found this to be an invaluable tool for marking how my time is used and how it can be better improved. I have also spent time going over my call sheets from the year prior figuring out where I can make better use of my time and be able to see more qualified prospects.

One of the other added benefits of planning tomorrow's workday before you go home today is that it allows you to relax and decompress from that day. I've always found I was mentally clear and able to leave work knowing I had done as much as I could and was prepared to start tomorrow with a clean slate.

When you are writing out what you are to do for the next day I take the ten most important things that I must personally do that day. The next step is I number those items from one to ten in order of importance with number one being first and number 10 being least important. I never go on to the number two task until I've completed the number one objective. This technique is something I learned through an Earl Nightingale program which he referred to as the $25,000 idea. I've never put a financial label on this technique for myself personally; however it has dramatically increased my productivity since I began applying it.

Always keep busy. There's always a little slow time when you can't call a prospect, keep busy during those times make your phone calls or do your paperwork. Always work the whole time you're working.

Average Salespeople spend their time:

90 % demonstrating
10 % everything else

Champions spend their time

40% presenting
10% prospecting
50% qualifying and planning

How do you start your day?

I start my day with the first two hours working on projects that are directly beneficial to my primary goal and objective. During this time I also listen to self-improvement audio programs and try to read something uplifting and inspirational. I spent years hitting the alarm clock, getting up and just rushing out to get to work. I found through personal experience I am a much more productive person when I start my day in a more beneficial manner. This way no matter what happens I know I have achieved something before most people have even woken up. I personally commit to 6-8 AM in the morning. I generally put in another hour after work as well. I work through lunch and work extra hours as well. Part of this discipline comes from the fact that I enjoy what I do for a living. I admit this is a rather extreme schedule for someone to commit to, however I have had a driving passion to grow and had a terrific amount of learning to do and material to work through. I noticed a change in my life by following this schedule. Within a year I published two books while working at least sixty hours a week, fulfilled the duties of an executor and listened to several hundred hours of audio instruction. I was also able to read many books, and synthesize this knowledge into something that was actionable. I also began actively sharing my knowledge with my sales team. I've always believed that if you want to learn something twice teach it once.

One hour a day on weekdays: Ensure that you are reading for one hour a day. That works out to approximately one book a week on average or 50 books a year. Remember the average North American reads less than three books per year. Commit to lifelong learning, take every seminar you can, read everything you get your hands on which will help you become a better salesperson. Take a blank sheet of paper and at the top of the page write your present primary goal clearly and simply. Next write down as many ideas as you can for improving the job in which you are employed. An hour a day, five days a week totals 260 hours a year. This increases your service six full extra working weeks a year, time devoted to thinking and planning, this alone will put you far above your competition.

Numbers: I've always tried to see a set number of customers daily. I believe that success is also a numbers game. The more you try, the more likely you are to triumph. I found that it helps to have a written prioritized list of who I'm going to call on prepared the night before. This is one of my daily rituals I use at the end of my workday it helps me focus and eliminate any worry that I may have missed something as well as decompress from that workday.

Top 10 time wasters:

1) Crisis management
2) Telephone interruptions
3) Lack of objectives and priorities planning
4) Attempting too much
5) Drop-in visitors
6) Ineffective delegation
7) Personal disorganization
8) Lack of self-discipline
9) Procrastination
10) Inability to say no

GOAL SETTING

"Goals are the fuel in the furnace of achievement." – *Brian Tracy*

The skill which is most important for you to cultivate on your path to becoming a sales professional is finding out what you want. If you really want something that desire will make a difference in your life.

Goal setting must be in writing, be specific and be believable.

The goal should be an exciting challenge, it should push you. Adjust as new information comes in. Your goals will help you guide your choices.

You should have two types of goals, long-term and short-term. Short-term goals should be no longer than 90 days and you should set goals in all areas of your life health, work, personal goals, family, spiritual life, etc.

Review your goals regularly, make them vivid. Set twenty-year goals, always have a future orientation, spend time visualizing what having your goals look like.

Have clear sales and income goals broken down into years, months, weeks, days and hours. For example I wanted to sell $1 million a year in newspaper ad space. To achieve this goal I worked backwards knowing my commission level I merely had to divide my goal by 50 weeks assuming a two week holiday and then I broke this total down by 40 hours. When I started thinking in terms of goals and objectives it changed how I utilized my time.

I also have the sales goals clearly described in written form. I thought of how much I want to earn and how much do I have to sell to accomplish that. I refer to these as often as possible.

FEAR

> "You gain strength, courage and confidence by every experience in which you really stop to look fear in the face. You are able to say to yourself, 'I have lived through this horror. I can take the next thing that comes along.' You must do the thing you think you cannot do."
> – *Eleanor Roosevelt*

Fear of failure and fear of rejection are the two biggest impediments to success in sales. Fear can strip you of your motivation. Focus on training and product knowledge and analyze your fears. Keep up to date on the latest methods and developments in your field. Get excited about what you're going to see and do.

One important component I would like to discuss in this book is fear. I don't know what your biggest fear will be but in terms of sales many people fear making a presentation, in dealing with cold calls and talking to people but by far the biggest fear I think that most salespeople face is the fear of rejection. Fear of rejection is the other side of the coin to the fear of failure. Rejection is the pathway to failure if you fear it.

Remember that failure actually only happens when you make the decision to quit. You can always choose your results, never quit, make sure you're looking at failure as an advance not a personal thing. Look for the reasons of why you might be failing and find the solutions not just blame, always list possible opportunities and ask yourself what you learned and try again. As long as you've learned something from it and made yourself better there's no such thing as failure.

You must develop the ability to go from one no to the next without losing your enthusiasm. Never allow one negative experience to spill over to the next customer interaction.

Psychologically one of the chief causes of failure is the expectancy of failure.

Learn what your fears are and then do what you fear most. Don't take rejection personally.

Overcome the fear of follow-through by knowing the business. You will find additional opportunities, analyze the call. What did you do that impressed the client? What could you have done better? What positive feelings did you engender? How can I use what I've learned to improve in the future?

When put in its proper place fear can be a good thing.

Overcoming fear of rejection:

The fear of rejection is one of the primary reasons salespeople fail. Society tells you that we must succeed, it must be great each and every time we undertake any activity at all. This can lead to negative thoughts, embarrassment, self-doubt and depression when rejected.

Allow yourself to be rejected, give yourself permission. This will allow you to be free. Once you give yourself this permission you can knock on any door, try any new thing, approach any customer and become more successful in not only sales but in all areas of your life. Rejection is a learning experience which can teach you about selling. If you don't make a sale figure out why. Rejection is not personal you are not judged by the number of times you fail but by the number of times you succeed and the number of times you succeed is in direct proportion to the number of times that you can fail and keep moving forward.

Never accept a no from someone who couldn't have given you a yes in the first place.

Demotivators:

Fear of losing security: If you refuse to give up anything that you have now where will the money, space, time and energy come from for new achievements.

Fear of failure if you do what you fear most you control the fear

Self-doubt

Pain of change: the pain of change is always forgotten when the benefits of that change are realized

Remember in selling, especially at the start activity breeds productivity, but it has to be busy doing the right things: keeping up with the industry, making presentations, lead generating activities, meeting new people, getting referrals and making appointments.

Worry:

The following is a breakdown of things that people worry about.

Things that never happened 40 %
Things over and past that can never be changed by all the worry in the world 30 %
Needless worries about our health 12 %
Petty miscellaneous worries 10 %
Real legitimate worries 8 %

92 percent of what an average person worries about, takes up valuable time causing stress when it was unnecessary. Instead focus on your goals and higher value activities.

One tool I have learned in my crisis intervention work which has proven to be extremely useful is what's called the 4-4-4-4 breath. This technique will lower your heart rate very quickly and allow you to regain composure. You begin inhaling for four seconds, hold that breath for four seconds, exhale for four seconds, hold the breath out for four seconds. Continue to do this breathing exercise for approximately 5 minutes and you will notice that you will feel incredibly calm and in control.

GOOD SALES HABITS AND SUGGESTIONS

"Ability is what you're capable of motivation determines what you
do an attitude determines how well you do it."
– Lou Holtz Notre Dame Coach.

- Feedback is the breakfast of champions and sales is certainly no exception. After every sales call I always ask myself what did I do right in this call? What would I do differently if I had that call to do over again?

- 75% of your time should be spent in the field working with qualified prospects. One of the so-called greatest secrets of sales is similar to the secret in real estate. The old rule of real estate was location, location, location. The sales version is see the people, see the people, and see the people. Although in this day and age we must take advantage of all technological advantages we must constantly hone our skills in face-to-face time with customers. Ever since I began in the sales industry I set myself a goal of seeing twenty people face to face every day. This is not always an easy goal to achieve with the amount of paperwork that is now involved in sales, however it is always been a worthy goal which has served me well. I do believe if you manage to see twenty people a day on most days your success in sales is almost ensured. Salespeople spend on average only 20% of their time face-to-face with customers. By increasing your face time with customers your sales will also increase.

- One of the things my dad always told me was that you could never go broke over servicing a customer. It important to listen to what is being asked and to really concentrate on building the relationship with the customer and to think like them.

- Always think positive. All of the great and successful people in history have had this trait. Great salespeople are no different.

- The exceptional salesperson does what the average salesperson won't.

- Think about reselling rather than single sales where you sell one time and never see the customer again. A customer today wants a relationship first. The relationship between you and your clients will affect sales. People will buy from the salesperson they like the most. They will then justify the decision based on this.

- Relationship management is important. Build them all of the time.

35

There is no room for high-pressure sales and manipulation anymore. The best salespeople are relationship and customer oriented. Don't do anything that will ruin the relationship. Study how customers buy, study their decision-making strategies and determine what their influences are. Build for long-term gain not short-term pleasures you want to shoot for relationships not gratification. Remember that nobody makes it on their own always try to help other people on their path to the sales industry as well.

- Listening builds trust.

- Emphasize the specific features and benefits of your product for the customer.
- What problems do my products solve?
- What benefit or service do we offer?

- Differentiate: What is my unique selling proposition?

- Position yourself as the best product rather than the lowest price. The customer will see you as the lowest risk, best choice provider of your service.

- Position yourself as an expert in your field.

- Enthusiasm will influence yourself and others

- Be reliable, dependable and honest

- Make sure you are selling for the long term. Sales should be long-term, relationship driven and referral oriented. You should not be thinking in terms of one offs. You should always try to build value into your interactions. There is no more room for sales manipulation or other underhanded tactics. Many salespeople have not respected this and the sales industry is taking a reputational hit because of it.

- Some of the biggest sales success strategies are believing that you will be successful. In that regard setting up the mental attitude to make sure you are successful as well as creating the right environment to make sure that everything is conducive to your success especially in your environment at work at home with your family and spouse etc.

- Networking is critical it's not always who you know it's who knows you. Always make sure that you're having the right associations with the right people, successful people. You want to make sure you're associating with the best people, go where the best customers and prospects go. You will want to stay away from poisonous people the ones that don't seem to go anywhere. Make sure you're mentoring a few people as well as being mentored yourself. Most of what I have to tell you in this book will not be a dramatic revelation but mostly simple strategies that will lead to sales success. The problem is that few people seem willing to do them which can be attributed to a lack of personal self discipline and dedication to lifelong learning without those two things everything else is very difficult.

- A big part of becoming a sales professional is personal responsibility, taking the personal responsibility and doing the work that's necessary to become a professional. Doing your homework, planning your days, managing your time and dealing with your customers with passion and knowledge and bringing value is what will make you successful in the sales field. Sales should be based on collaboration never manipulation. People want to partner with others not just deal with salespeople.

- Decide to be successful. Take any training that improves your communication skills or people skills. Any time or effort spent on bettering yourself will always pay dividends. A good habit of success in the sales industry is always thinking about prospecting, spending more and more time with better prospects and spending time looking for new business. The only time to really ever relax in prospecting is when you have so many customers that you don't have enough time to sell and satisfy all the people who want to buy from you.

- Think about things that you can do every day to make your products and services more attractive to your customers.

- Role-plays are important also, you should commit to regular practice and reading one hour of study per day in your field and you will be amazed at the difference you'll see in yourself. One of the biggest advantages in a career in sales that you are always learning and learning new things with your customers business.

- I've had the great fortune to interact and learn from hundreds of clients. This exposure to a diverse array of clients has also allowed me to get tips from people. No two clients think or act the same way. I have taken some of the best of what I've learned from them and incorporated them into my life.

- The golden rule applies to everyone.

- The secret to success is to subjugate your ego and serve others.

- Specialized knowledge of the customer and their situation can be important. Your knowledge of the customer's business: How does it work? Where's the profit made? How can you improve that profit and how they make their living what are their other problems and concerns and what are their plans or you know about the customer the better you can serve them.

- High quality relationships built on trust represents more than 40% of the sale.

- Database your experience and knowledge. Know the variances and where they can improve what your customers are doing? What are their customers doing? This is what separates you from your competitor, how can you increase your customers output? What areas can my product offer the greatest difference?

- Position yourself as an advisor to the customer. You want them to come to you with their concerns. Follow up and ask how is it working, by how much is it working, quantify it. Calculate the true worth of your product and the return on investment write it down for the. Always look for opportunities to do this process again and again.

- Reputation is your most valuable asset. How they talk about you and think about you when you're not there?

- Resales the first sale is always expensive to get. Resales are cheaper. A customer has already received satisfaction from your product is easier to make follow-up sales referrals should be the main source of new business rates the best salespeople are the best at prospecting even though they don't have to any.

- Specialization. Self-knowledge what have you done in the past that accounts for most of your success? What kind of customers do you sell easily to?

- Company knowledge: Ensure you know your company business backwards and forwards no question should ever stump you.

- Competitors knowledge what are their strengths why are you losing sales to them?

- Cost and sales structures of customers industry what makes your customers tick how does their cash flow work?

- Decision-making and buying decisions. Who is the person to talk to? This is a critical area.

- Call someone in a different department and get to know the company. Check the company at the Chamber of Commerce, always do your research. Planning can improve your chances of a sale by more than 80%.

- The amateur practices until they get it right. Professionals practice until they never get it wrong.

- Consulting and trouble-shooter is the way a customer should see you not just as a vendor of services.

- Get out of yourself and start thinking like the customer find the problems the customer has that are profitable to solve.

- Every sales failure is usually a result of you not demonstrating that the value of the product or service is far more than the cost.

- Sales can be tough because you get up every day and face inevitable rejection. Commit to continually sharpening your skills and commit to being in the top 10% of this industry.

- The law of cause and effect is crucial in sales. Look at what the most successful salespeople are doing and do what they do.

- I've always been a firm believer in getting to know as many people in a company as possible. With what my car dealers in addition to the buyer and main decision-maker I been able to meet the mechanics the financing people as well as the sales staff and I found this really increases my knowledge of their business and allows me to serve them even better.

- Always tell the truth. Sales is about building bridges and building rapport.

- Always tell people what you do for a living, where you work and what you sell. Never be ashamed of what you do for a living. Always take pride in what you do knowing that you're helping businesses grow.

- Always do your best when you sell and stick to your principles is nothing more dangerous than a salesperson with the wrong attitude. It's dangerous to both customers and to the salesperson themselves also your responsibility to the industry that were all in and I've never been a fan of people who further ridiculous stereotypes about the sales profession is treated me so very well.

- Establish a customer need. Never lie to a prospect. Always listen to what the prospect has to say. Carry a positive mental attitude and commit to ongoing professional development.

- Do your homework. Always be prepared before going to see a prospect. Research them on the Internet look up their sites, Google them and use other search engines as well and see what comes up, take notes. Also Google the name of the CEO and look up the name of the person you're meeting and look through any of their company literature. Also talk to their vendors if possible find out what it's like to do business with them ask if they pay on time and any other information you get is also good to talk to their competition, talk to their customers talk to people that you may already know that also may know them talk to some other employees talk to their sales department. Also Google yourself and see what comes up is you got to be sure that your competition is probably doing that as well.

- Always remember that there is homework involved in sales and that your day always starts the night before. The most successful salespeople do their preparation, turn the TV off and do your homework. I know this is a lot of extra work however it's one of the biggest mistakes in sales trying to wing it and not having a proper plan.

- Never overwhelm a customer with too many choices. Too many choices leave them to be unable to make a choice.

- Sales is not merely having the gift of the gab. Most people think they need to talk, talk, and talk. It is actually the opposite. You need to ask your customers more questions and listen!!! Learn from the experts and do what other successful sales people do over and over again and get good at it and you will get the same results.

- Always present the emotion first, logic second. The sequence is important want and desire first and then following up with logic works extremely well. People buy first with their hearts and later justify with their heads.

Although some of the tips may seem repetitive they bear repeating because they are important in the sales industry.

CONTINUOUS LEARNING

"The purpose of learning is growth, and our minds, unlike our bodies, can continue growing as long as we live." – Mortimer Adler

There is never an end to the training for people involved in the sales industry. It is a position of ongoing education and continual self-improvement. A lot of sales reps that I've worked with have really hated performing role plays. I have found role-playing to be an important place to provide you with an opportunity and arena for you to make errors. Mistakes we make in the office cost us no money as opposed to losing a potential sale. While I was employed as a class facilitator in crisis intervention and conflict resolution of the crisis line one of the primary tools we utilized to prepare a phone line volunteer to perform the role of a crisis worker was role-plays. I would strongly encourage any new sales rep to spend the first six months role-playing for 30 minutes a day. Great sales reps are a lot like professional athletes they practice, practice, practice.

Learning on a continuous basis is necessary in life and in sales. You should always be researching new things that can be applied to your career. Don't limit yourself to only reading in your field, engage your creativity. Turn the TV off and read for an hour every day in your field. Work on your communication skills. I have included resources in the back of this book to help you grow even further.

Read in your field for 30 to 60 minutes each day and think throughout the day of how you can use what you've learned if you do that each day you should be completing one book per week. The average North American reads less than three books per year. If you read one book per week you should finish at least 50 books each year. Earning a PhD from a major university requires the reading and synthesis into a dissertation of about 40 to 50 books.

The average person spends 500 to 1000 hours each year in his or her vehicle. This is the equivalent of 3 to 6 months of 40 hour weeks or the equivalent of one or two university semesters. Make sure you're using this time to your best advantage by listening to audio programs in your vehicle.

Learn the 80/20 principle. It is critical in sales as well as other endeavours. 20% of your clients will account for 80% of your income. You should be spending more time with these types of clients.

Keep bettering yourself. What got you here isn't good enough. Spend the time learning new skills, coming up with creative ideas always working on bettering yourself. Remember that school is never out for the professional salesperson.

Self esteem:

Self-esteem is important because as a salesperson you will never perform any better then you believe that you are capable of being. I have also included some affirmations for increasing self esteem in the appendix section. If you read these out loud several times a day, you will find yourself noticing the effects.

Tools for Sales People

1) Testimonials what are other people saying about your service?

These can take the form of
      a) Letters
      b) List of existing customers
      c) Photos of people you've worked with

2) The number of referrals or resales you get.

3) Third-party endorsements.

These show that your product works and it lowers perceived risk. The satisfied customer by far is the finest advertising in the world.

SALES ETIQUETTE AND APPEARANCE

> "You never get a second chance to make a good first impression"
> – *Will Rogers*

First impressions are of major importance. Be aware of your appearance at all times including the vehicle you drive, the clothes you wear, and the manner of speech you use. The salesperson who dresses immaculately creates the image of an efficient well polished and confident individual. Always use your best manners.

The way you see yourself determines how others will see you. People will see you how you see yourself. All the top salespeople see themselves in three ways:

1) See yourself as a consultant not a salesperson. You are a problem solver.

2) See themselves as doctors of selling. They are professionals they do a diagnosis and offer a prescription. The differences you will make a house call.

3) See yourself as the president of the company don't complain or badmouth people. Take ownership and be responsible for your success. Dress the part, act the part.

Never be late for an appointment- Be Punctual: Being late shows disrespect. Being early more than 5 minutes shows you don't have anything better to do or that you're anxious.

Smile: A friendly face is more pleasant than a grim one

Shake Hands: Make your grip firm and confident and pump no more than 3 times. Look the other person in the eye and smile. Stand 3-4 feet away: Get closer and you'll make the other person feel uncomfortable. Farther away and you'll appear detached and disinterested. The secret of a successful handshake: Go for the Web: Facing the person directly, extend your hand with your thumb up so you can lock the web of your thumb with the other persons. If someone grabs you by the fingers try to slip your hand in further. Give a couple of shakes from the elbow.

Maintain Eye Contact: If you don't many people feel that you are lying or not dependable. Don't wear dark glasses

Shut the door on your troubles. Avoid any discussions of your family or financial troubles. Think about what you can do for the customer.

Speaking voice:

To achieve a perfect blend of oxygenation and oration:

Relax your Jaw: You can enrich your speaking voice by keeping your jaw relaxed. There should be a little cushion of air between the top and bottom teeth. Think of your tongue belonging to the bottom of the jaw, rather than just being stuck in there. Always have a half-yawn in the back of your mouth so there's room for the sound to come out over the back of your tongue. Clarity and articulation command respect. Be assertive not aggressive when speaking. You want to get rid of the noise in your voice. You want more depth, amplification, resonance. It's more like singing than speaking which is exactly what you must do develop this skill. The more music in your voice, the less noise in your voice.

Be attentive to body language: Avoid raising barriers. Don't cross your arms across your chest. Don't place anything on the desk between you and the interviewer. Avoid the appearance of withdrawing from the interviewer.

Be calm and poised: avoid nervous habits. Don't cross your legs and keep the free moving. Don't play with your fingernails, keep your hands off your moustache, beard and/or hair, don't play with jewellery, and don't tap your finger on the chair arm or table. Sit up straight, don't slouch and avoid aggravating speech habits such as eh!

- Never chew gum or eat when talking to a customer

- Never smoke while making sales call

- No off-color jokes discussions about religion politics or race

- Always look your customer in the eye

- Listen!!

- Always thank the customer for their time.

- Smile

The value of a smile:

It costs nothing but creates much,
It enriches those who receive it without impoverishing those who give it,
It happens in a flash and the memory of it sometimes lasts forever.

None are so rich that they get along without it.

It creates happiness at the home, fosters goodwill in business and is the countersign of friends.

It is rest to the weary, daylight to the discouraged, sunshine to the sad and nature's best antidote for trouble.

Yet it can't be bought, begged, borrowed or stolen, for it is something that is no earthly good to anyone until it is given away.

And if we are too tired to give you a smile may we ask that you leave one of yours, for nobody needs a smile as much as those who have none left to give.

Author unknown

THE 10 SINS OF SALES

> "The customer may not always be right, but the customer is *always* the customer" – *Dr. Phil Littlewood*

1) I don't know: customers expect you know your products and services there is no reason for you not to know you should know your own company forward and backwards.

2) I know it all: not letting a customer finish speaking before jumping in to offer a solution is being pushy you may know the answer but make sure the customer is ready to hear it.

3) I'm right and you're wrong: arguing with a customer. The customer may not always be right however it doesn't cost anything to give them the benefit of the doubt.

4) Hurry up and wait: respect your customers time and they will respect you in return.

5) I don't care: when your attitude, communications or appearance says you'd rather be someplace else, the customer will be wishing the same thing and will take their business elsewhere.

6) You don't know anything: there are no dumb questions or dumb answers. Verbally cutting off customers slams the door in their face and they will find a better door to walk into next time.

7) Biases and prejudices: check them at the door before you start work. Be aware of them. People want to be treated fairly and they deserve to.

8) Thou does not need to prepare. Always prepare to help your clients. Proper planning prevents poor performance.

9) Lack of passion.

10) Don't come back: you provide value and good service so they come back and they also will tell their friends and family. Thanking customers for their patronage and loyalty builds customer service, letting the customer know they are valued. To fail to do so is to invite failure.

Business mistakes:

1) The downward spiral trap: cutting your marketing budget/advertising

budget when things get tough.
2) Competitor fixation: you should not be fixated on what your
   competitors are doing. You should be aware of what they're doing,
   however, fixate on the customer instead.
3) Internal strife
4) Failure to reinvest in yourself and your company.
5) Hubris, thinking the good times will never end and every thing is always
   going to be fantastic.

Comfort zone:

I used to have a comfort zone where I knew I could not fail.
The same four walls and busy work were really more like jail.
I longed so much to do the things I've never done before.
But I stayed inside my comfort zone and paced the same old floor.

I said it didn't matter that I wasn't doing much.
I said I didn't care for things like diamonds, cars and such.
I claim to be so busy with the things inside my zone.
But deep inside I longed for some victory of my own.

I couldn't let my life go by.
Just watching others win
I held my breath and stepped outside to let the change begin.
I took a step and with a strain I'd never felt before.
I kissed my comfort zone goodbye and closed and locked the door.

If you're in a comfort zone afraid to venture out
Remember that all winners at one time were filled with doubt
A step or two and words of praise can make your dreams come true
So greet your future with a smile, success is there for you.

Author unknown

SLUMPS

Every once in a while every salesperson gets down, I know I did. I also realize I don't sell as much when I'm not busy. When I realize I feel a bit down I try to immediately shift my thinking back to my motivations. I think about what my clients need and how they require the best of me. I also have financial thoughts that I do need money which allows me to get what I need. I do find I make money in direct proportion to the level of service I bring to my clients. Other motivators are security, achievement, recognition, acceptance by others, self acceptance and family.

Sometimes you will get into a slump in sales, it has happened to me. I found that one of the best things to do is fall back on the good habits that you've already built. Some people say take a holiday for me I've always went out on a call that I knew I could close with no real problem just to instill a sense of enthusiasm.

When you're in a bad mood or negative people can sense that. The customer will often play into that negativity and that's just the time to go back to basics and work with the client. Sell something easy and simple, one that you could do with your hands tied behind your back, and something that will restore your confidence and get rid of that negative attitude turning it into a positive one.

You should be making contact with people on your list at least every 90 days.

Remember Luck: Good luck comes when preparedness and opportunity meet. Keep positive and you will start finding luck.

Make sure you enjoy the present. I spent so much time working and heading towards things I stopped enjoying the process. Whatever you're looking for must be found within you first whether it's riches, peace or happiness. Emerson said "though we travel the world over to find the beautiful, we must carry it within us or we will find it not."

You become what you think about. Fill your mind with thoughts of achieving goals instead of negativity.

You should focus more on what selling is about which is providing solutions and benefits to customers needs.

PERSISTENCE

When I originally started in newspaper sales advertising I did more than 500 face to face cold calls in less than three weeks. I started out as a very enthusiastic young rep. It was not long before I started to get worn down and I began to think that sales might not be the career for me. I faced a fair bit of rejection which led me to think I was in the wrong business. When I spoke with a new rep I started to think about this time of my career and at the time I hated this portion but I realized later how much of a valuable experience it was for me. I learned a lot about myself and originally when I was questioning my career choices my dad, who had been in sales for years said it was important not to take it personally. He reaffirmed that some customers said no because it wasn't the right time for their business, they had yet to see the value, it had not been budgeted for, as well as several other possible reasons. After those three weeks however all the yeses started to roll in and my career was off to a running start. I used to resent this time but I don't think there's anything that can replace that kind of experience and I wouldn't trade it for anything because the salesperson I eventually became was really forged during that period.

Often when you think you can't do anymore and you feel discouraged and want to quit this is often the time when you break through to great achievements. Ralph Waldo Emerson said when the night is darkest the stars come out.

Don't quit

When things go wrong, as they sometimes will,
when the road you're trudging seems all uphill,
when the funds are low and the debts are high,
and you want to smile but you have to sigh,
when care is pressing you down a bit - rest if you must,
but don't you quit.
Life is queer with its twists and turns.
As everyone of us sometimes learns.
And many a fellow turns about when he might have won had he stuck it
out.
Don't give up though the pace seems slow - you may succeed with another
blow.
Often the goal is nearer than it seems to a faint and faltering man;
often the struggler has given up when he might have captured the victor's
cup;
and he learned too late when the night came down,
how close he was to the golden crown.
Success is failure turned inside out - the silver tint of the clouds of doubt,
and when you never can tell how close you are,
it may be near when it seems afar;
so stick to the fight when you're hardest hit - it's when things seem worst,
you must not quit.

Author unknown

CONCLUSION

There are a lot of careers in sales from door-to-door sales to phone sales. I have never found someone in sales that could not use extra tools and a little more knowledge to help hone what it is that they do. I'm hoping that this book will help be one of those tools and I've also included several others in the resource section for you to take your sales education that much further.

One lesson I had to learn the hard way was to take time for yourself, and to take a break. You don't want to run yourself right down, as sales is a profession in which you need to take the long view and realize that an occasional mistake today doesn't mean that it's going to happen forever. Trend is not destiny

Remember lighten up as well and don't lose control of the fact that you're the one in charge of your day, your mind and your career. You're the one that people come to for your answers to solve their problems. Keep your head, ask good questions and be precise when it comes to giving good advice. Success happens more often to the person with a positive mental attitude.

Never cut corners at the expense of your own credibility it is your most powerful tool. Develop leadership skills and focus on building mutually beneficial long-term partnerships.

People talk about the natural born salesperson. It is a myth because although some people may be born with certain attributes that make them successful in sales, there is no person who can't improve upon their skills to become a true sales champion. This information will help you achieve the ability to move into the top 5 to 10% of your industry. It will take some work to get there. There is a lot of knowledge to be learned and practiced. Give it total commitment and make it a part of yourself and it will serve you well in your career. I think there's a huge difference in knowing what to do and in doing it. This book will provide you with tools to help you grow but it's not going to do the work for you. It's up to you to take that personal responsibility and grow as a person and as a sales representative becoming the true professional that I know you're capable of becoming.

Learn about customer service don't just be a smooth talking salesman. We don't want robots that have memorized hundreds of speeches, practice empathy and never use deception

My dad always told me there is no such thing as a wasted sales call. I've always found this to be true. Many times I have went in and not made a sale that day but learned something else, improved my skills, got a referral, or in some other way was able to improve what I do.

One of the corporate vice presidents I worked for when I began working in this business used to always tell me to take the high road. He said that so often that it became a mantra. I heard it so many times that whenever I would actually have a decision this was always in my mind. This advice has always stood me in good stead and has partially been responsible for my success.

Mental attitude, good work habits and professionalism will help you cross the line to becoming a successful salesperson. Sales offers freedom, opportunity, success, challenge, fun and satisfaction. You must not only read this book, you must consume it, practice what it contains, reread it. Becoming a sales professional is a process. Sales can lead to a lifetime of prosperity and security. It will allow you to make a living helping other people achieve their goals, there is no better feeling.

This book has many concepts and techniques that will help you have a more fulfilling experience in sales and life in general. This will make you happier which will have a noticeable effect on both you and your loved ones. You can become a sales professional and achieve all of your dreams and goals through selling. I look forward to your success and am excited to have played a small part in it. I welcome the opportunity to hear from you and I can be contacted at krispatterson99@gmail.com.

Always keep your sense of humour.

Good luck and great selling!!

ACKNOWLEDGEMENTS

Many people have helped me with this book and encouraged me along the way. I have spoken with my clients to discuss my thoughts on the creation of this book and they have all agreed to its necessity. My clients range from car dealers to realtors to restaurants to clothing stores to electronic shops and all other forms of retail and they have all seen the need for such a book. This is the fourth book I've published but the first to specifically deal with sales.

As with all of my book projects, the credit goes to Phil Littlewood. He has helped me immensely and helped me to discover my message and bring it to reality. I never would have been able to create these projects without him. Phil and his wife Amie are more than just friends; they are a source of support for me in my life and have been through some of the darkest periods of my life. There are no words to express my gratitude towards Phil and Amie.

I would also like to thank Chris Finlayson for being my guinea pig and allowing me to bounce ideas off of him. I've spent lots of time learning to systematically work on the sales process. I investigated what worked and what didn't and more importantly how can I transfer what worked to allow it to work for someone else. Chris has also graciously written the foreword for this book and he's also one of the new sales reps who were part of my motivation for creating this book.

FURTHER EDUCATION:

Through a combination of my reading, experience on thousands of sales calls, as well as my experiences firsthand and secondhand through my father's experience and other people's anecdotes I have attempted to gather the best tools I can find to help people increase their sales ability.

One of the best educational experiences I've had with regard to skill in sales was actually a course offered by North Island College called customer service excellence. This program although having nothing to do with sales was all based on ensuring the best customer experience. The skills that the course offered were directly applicable to sales and I use them daily in my career. It solely focused on building rapport and communication skills especially by asking open-ended questions and working on active listening these are also some of the same skills that I learned during my four years in crisis intervention. The difference is in crisis intervention stakes are a lot higher if you make mistakes. This period of my life is where I really started to hone my skills. I very proud of some of the differences I made while working in that industry and it became part of me which I of course brought forward into my sales career.

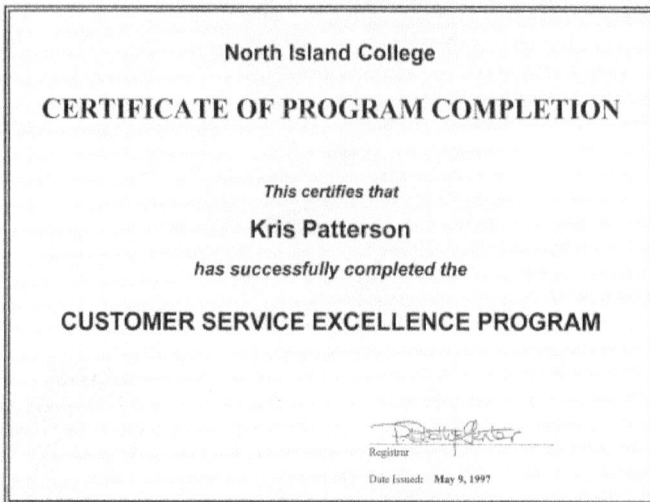

North Island College

CERTIFICATE OF PROGRAM COMPLETION

This certifies that

Kris Patterson

has successfully completed the

CUSTOMER SERVICE EXCELLENCE PROGRAM

Registrar

Date Issued: May 9, 1997

Certificate of Completion for Customer Service Excellence Course

With communication being as important as it is, in life and sales, I would strongly encourage you to invest the time in joining a Toastmaster group. There are many groups and you can find the nearest one to you by going to toastmaster.org they offer 90 minutes of evaluated practice every week. This will improve your speaking skills and will lead to innumerable other benefits.

Psychology is also an important part of sales. Learning more about what motivates people and what motivates yourself will go a long way to helping you and your sales career. I completed a diploma in adult psychology as well as one in child psychology this has helped me in my career both as the salesperson and other aspects of my working life.

International Career School Canada

This certifies that

KRIS PATTERSON

has successfully completed a comprehensive program in

CHILD PSYCHOLOGY

and, in recognition thereof, is hereby awarded this

Diploma
WITH HIGHEST HONOURS

In witness whereof, we have hereto subscribed our names and affixed the seal of the institution at Montreal, Quebec, on this 18th day of March A.D. 2009

David Smith
Director of Education

Connie C. Dempsey
Chief Academic Officer

I completed a second diploma in child psychology.

Diploma in Adult Psychology a subject which has always interested me

I originally completed my diploma in Adult Psychology and had more to learn so I went back and completed one in Child Psychology as well. It is important to always be learning and improving.

I've been very fortunate to be introduced to Peter Lamb and his philosophy of sales through my career at the newspaper. He is one of the facilitators who are returning things to a more customer service focus in sales. I would encourage you to seek him out on YouTube and attend one of his events.

RESOURCES

The following are some books, programs I found useful in my career.

Books and Audio Programs

To Sell Is Human: by Daniel Pink. This book really is a great example of the new sales world. I recommend everyone read this book, at least once. I have this as an audio book and it is one the programs I listen to while driving.

Think and grow Rich Napoleon Hill

Lead the Field and the Strangest Secret Earl Nightingale

Advanced selling Brian Tracy

The greatest salesman in the world Og Mandino

The war of Art by Stephen Pressfield

The art of exceptional living by Jim Rohn

The Accidental Salesperson: Chris Lytle

Strengths based selling: Tony Rutigliano and Brian Brim

I also read Success Magazine every month. I found it offers a lot of great material and each issue includes an audio CD with added content.

SUPPLEMENTAL INFO

10 Keys to success in sales by Brian Tracy

1) Learn to love your work and commit to be the very best at what you do

2) Decide exactly what you want in life and decide the price you are going to pay for it set the goal write it down

3) Back every goal with persistence and determination

4) Commit yourself to lifelong learning read books, listen to tapes, and attend seminars the more knowledge we take in the more our rewards can grow.

5) Use your time wisely what is the most valuable use of my time right now always ask yourself that.

6) Follow the leaders

7) Guard your integrity as if it is a sacred thing

8) Treat every prospect well

9 Use your inborn creativity

10) Work hard and you will succeed

10 STEPS TO STOP PROCRASTINATING

1) List what you are putting off

2) Do one task right away

3) Set designated time to start task

4) Beat boredom by using your mind

5) Imagine you have only one year to live

6) Don't worry about perfection

7) Say "I will"

8) If what you are putting off involves other people, consult with them

9) If your fear the consequences for the action, ask yourself what is the very worst thing can happen

10) Vividly picture how free you will feel once the task is completed

Nine steps to problem solving:

1) Define the problem

2) Write down everything you know about the problem

3) Decide what people and resources to bring into the solution

4) Make a note of everything that is related to the problem

5) Conduct a brainstorming session by yourself

6) Conduct a brainstorming session in a group

7) Evaluate the ideas for the best options

8) Create an action plan

9) Give yourself a deadline to put the plan into action.

Seven Keys to persuasiveness:

1) Ask the right person

2) Ask at the right time

3) Use the right offer

4) Have the right evidence

5) Have the right answers

6) Have the right strategy

7) Ask with the right attitude

AFFIRMATIONS FOR BUILDING SELF-ESTEEM

1. I am a valuable person and worthy of the respect of others.

2. I am optimistic about life! I look forward to and enjoy new challenges to my awareness

3. I am my own expert and I allow others the same privilege.

4. I express my ideas easily and I know that there are others who respect my point of view

5. I am aware of my values and confident in the decisions I make based on my awareness

6. I have pride in my past performance and a positive expectancy for the future

7. I bounce back quickly from disappointments

8. I can accept compliments and I can share success

9. I am a unique and therefore precious being

10. I am actively in charge of my life and I direct it in constructive channels

11. I realize that love is letting go of fear and grievances

12. It is not what happens to me but how I handle it that determines my emotional well being.

13. I love myself, and like myself, I am ok

14. I am an action person, doing first things first and one thing at a time

15. I treat everyone with warmth and respect.

16. I am gentle with myself

17. I can make mistakes and still remain a valuable and worthwhile person

18. I forgive myself and others easily

19. I am responsible for the way I see and react to the world around me

20. I feel strong, competent and capable

13 EFFECTIVE NETWORKING TIPS

Networking starts at home

All contacts are important

Have your contact introduce you

Prepare for each meeting

Keep careful notes

Join an organization

Go to social and business events

Volunteer

Leave a resume

Collect business cards

Don't accept everything you hear

Show appreciation

Be yourself

USEFUL TELEPHONE TECHNIQUES

Arrange the proper environment (location/distraction/comfort)

Prepare for telephone use (personal appointment book/available times/paper/pen)

Prepare for each call on paper (this will focus your attention)

Prepare and use a good opening statement (to attract the attention of your prospect)

Prepare questions in advance

Practice your delivery several times before key calls. Use a tape to improve delivery, find flaws, and gain confidence

Maintain a positive attitude (I will be successful in achieving my objective)

Use more than normal voice inflection and smile during the calls (this will convey your real enthusiasm)

Take notes (focuses your attention and provides a record of the call)

Make several calls at one time (saves time and maintains consistent phone delivery and builds momentum)

Give alternate choices for appointments and be available whenever it is convenient for the other

At the end of each call make sure the person knows how to reach you

Keep a list of who you called and when

Remember each call you make, especially when you are first starting out, you are going to learn something. The more you do the better you'll get

HOW TO GET PAST THE SECRETARIAL BLOCKADE

Always know whom you are calling: just as you would never right a blind letter to a company, never call without knowing the person's full name. You can use company operators to find out names and accurate spelling for follow-up letters. Ask the switchboard operator for the phone number that will put you directly in touch with the person who has the final decision on hiring (as a general rule the head of the department or the supervisor.

Phone before or after normal working hours: an effective way of getting around secretaries and assistants is to call before 9:00 am or after 5:00 pm most secretaries work 9-5. An early or later call usually catches the department head answering their own phones.

Don't tell the secretary the call is personal: you'll get connected all right but the person may resent your invasion of his/her privacy.

He or she is busy or absent: if the person is busy or absent ask to speak to him his/her replacement or to an assistant. If unable to do so ask what hours the person will be available.

Try and try again: don't leave your name and phone number. Tell him/her you're planning to be away and will call back. This keeps initiative on your side.

I'm sorry he or she is unable to see you at this time: if you are unable to speak to the person who does the hiring ask the secretary if you can go down and fill out an application form.

What's this in reference to? Or can I help you? When he/she says: can I help you instead of saying no say yes perhaps you can? I am interested in knowing what kind of sampling techniques you will use...' or some other technical point. If he or she does know the answer, thank him/her and ask if you can talk to his or her boss (use the person's name) about it and if this isn't a convenient time then when would be?

Always be polite with the secretary.

TIPS FOR SALES MANAGERS

Sales meetings should always be Monday morning 9 AM.

The first 15 minutes: the sales reps should share success stories from last week.

The meeting should never last more than an hour.

Sales numbers should be discussed for 15 minutes.

Any promotions that are coming up should be discussed at these meetings.

The last 15 minutes of the meeting should be reserved for training.

The two things you should leave a meeting with is a shot in the arm and a little bit of tools and wisdom you can use for your sales week ahead a good sales manager should be preparing his agenda and information for the meetings Sunday nights before the Monday sales meeting the last five minutes of every meeting should end with role players.

Debrief salespeople's calls tell them you will be asking certain questions so that they will know what you will be asking. This will focus the rep's attention assuring that they get the questions from the customer that you would like to know for example what was the result of the call when does the rep call on them again etc.

This Was Then...
With Old Ike

A Collection of
excerpts from Ike's
"This Was Then..."
column

Edited
& compiled
Kris Patterson

I Will Always Love You Ella

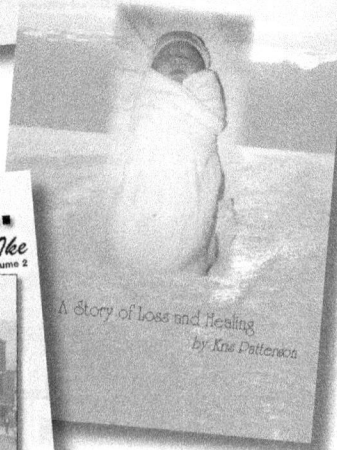

A Story of Loss and Healing
by Kris Patterson

This Was Then...
With Old Ike
Volume 2

Another Collection of
excerpts from Ike's
"This Was Then..."
column

Edited
& compiled by
Kris Patterson

Other Titles by
Kris Patterson